MINIMALISM

how living with less makes life whole

by Valentina Palermo V.

_____

To my family, who are still confused about how
I can travel for months with just a carry on.

_____

CONTENT

INTRODUCTION

What is the meaning of life? This might be an extremely complex question to answer even for someone who has lived long enough to realize what really matters and what is important in this life. Finding out what the meaning of life is could take a lifetime. There's no certain one answer, and people who do find out appear to do so approaching the end of their lives.

Well, whatever it is you're not going to find it laying around in your clutter. No, it isn't hiding inside that new car or computer either. Instead of searching for the meaning of life, strive to make your life meaningful.

This book is going to look at very different areas of your life. I believe that you must reevaluate your choices and apply new knowledge to all of them if you want a significant change. Areas such as health and finance which are not alway included in minimalism books are articles will be talked about a lot. Specifically, this book is going to be a little bit heavy on the money and finance side, I apologize about that if that's not what you're looking for but it is a topic I'm very passionate about since I believe has the biggest chance to impact your life positively. It might seem like it's a bit off topic at times, however I have seen that most minimalists improve their financials massively when they adopt this lifestyle so even though it might be a topic most books don't focus on I believe it is essential to include it.

Of course we are also going to go through the spiritual and psychological sides of minimalism in order to give you an integral guide on how this can impact your life.

The only way to achieve massive change is to take massive action and the only one who can do that is you. Have no mercy when getting rid of those things which are just taking away your time and money while not adding happiness to your life.

*Disclaimer: I am not a certified professional in finance, nutrition, health or any other topic. The advice in this book is from personal experience. Talk to a professional if you're planning to make a big change in your life so that you can get proper advice and guidance.

*This book contains two affiliate links related to the topics that are discussed, which means if you click on them I will get a commission.

CHAPTER 1: MISCONCEPTIONS

"Life is simple but we insist on making it complicated."

- Confucius

Depending on where you grew up you have a certain preconception of how things are supposed to work out and how life is supposed to be lived. What success is supposed to look like and what being rich means. You probably experience pressure from your family to get a degree, have a family, buy a house. This pressure never really ends and it is originated from a place of love. Your family only wants the best from you and that is alright. You should only want the best for yourself as well. Of course, no one apart from you can know what your dream life is like.

Most people we look at and think they're doing well are actually either in debt or living paycheck to paycheck, which can be extremely dangerous as you become dependent on your income and can't afford to lose your job or quit it. It is astonishing to see the amount of people who didn't manage to save enough for retirement and now rely on the government or their family to help support them. Imagine not being able to support yourself after a life of hard work. It must not only feel awful to have no control over your income, but also to realize that you spent on stuff that didn't give anything back to you. That extra money you have at the end of the month shouldn't be used to buy new clothes and gadgets, it should go to investments that will help you secure your future.

Whether you choose to invest in the stock market, in real estate or anything else is up to you. But the responsibility to make your investments work is all yours, so pick an industry you either know or that you plan to understand. I want you to be successful, to be in control of your life. I want you to be able to help your family if they ever got into this situation.

America in general has got an extremely consumerist mindset, in which more equals better. Driven by greed, people never seem to be satisfied. This can be seen even in the meals they serve you when you go out to a restaurant. Portions seem to be for at least two people and I'm sure you could feed four if those people are used to having small meals. The kids meal is the size of an adult's meal in other countries, believe me as I have seen it. Meals are probably even three times the size of meals in Europe. Americans in general live better than most people around the world, yet there's always that need to have more and more. And I'm not even referring to self development, we want more stuff! We don't want to be kinder, smarter, more helpful, we want to have the latest gadgets, a bigger house and more and newer cars. Greed is a trap, don't fall for it.

I see one message everywhere: consume, consume, consume. It is in all categories as well, food, media, information, products, classes, education, advice, etc. Everyone tells you to consume as much as possible but no one tells you that you should be discriminating what you consume. If you consume too many news about shootings and terrorism, you become afraid of what could happen because your body takes that fear and interprets it as if you were the one going through that stuff. If you take advice from broke people on how to become a millionaire, guess what? You'll most likely end up broke.

Before taking advice from anyone make sure they know what they're talking about and they apply it in their lives. One of the best advice I've been given is to not take advice from anyone whose life you wouldn't like to have. What does this mean? That if their relationship with their spouse is incredible, you should be asking for relationship advice. While if they have already declared bankruptcy on two businesses and can't pay the bills most months you shouldn't be asking or accepting advice on how yo manage a business and money. The best part is that you can take advice on just one topic from each different person, so if there's something admirable about their lives you can just ask them about it. Also, we have a huge advantage now that we have access to the internet most of the time in the sense that before, you could only get a mentor by finding him or her and spending a lot of time together learning. While now you can just go to Youtube and find thousands of videos of people like Tony Robbins or Elon Musk. It almost feels as if you were having a one on one conversation with them when you see their interviews. Find someone you admire and look for content created by them or with them in it, learn how they think and figure out what the reason of their success is.

Another important topic is that you should be a little skeptical of what you hear. Some people give talks about how real estate is the best way to get rich after writing a book on it, and the reality is that they actually got rich (or acquired a huge chunk of their wealth) from the sales of the books, courses and all the other merchandise surrounding the product. This doesn't mean the advice on the book is not valid, you could get rich from real estate no doubt, but just be aware of situations like that in which they portray one solution as the end all be all when in reality there's a whole lot going on that we have no way to be aware of. So what happens here is that they're not really giving you the recipe for their success, but rather what selling you one way to acquire wealth which isn't the one they used.

Everyone is trying to sell you something. It is your duty to protect yourself from purchasing those things that will end up being a dead weight to carry in your life. I can't even watch TV in this country without wanting to buy everything they show, that's how good marketing is, specially in the U.S..

I don't know if you've noticed but everywhere you look, there's ads. If you're driving on the highway you see ads. When you're looking at your social media there's ads again, which is fantastic if you're a business owner since you have access to a target market that's already segmented because of the information they put on their profiles but not if you're a user unless publicity has no effect on you. If you're walking in the city there's ads everywhere, even at churches. The enemy is not marketing, marketing is essential for the health of a business and it also injects a lot of money into the economy as it is usually expensive but worth it. However, since this book is about minimalism, this predominance of ads everywhere in our lives seems counterproductive. Developing the skill or discipline to not be tempted by ads can be done but it takes a bit of time, specially if you're a recovering consumerist.

Minimalism is not about depriving yourself, that should be clear from the start. It is about having enough and avoiding excess, because not even water in excess is good. Whoever tries to give minimalism a bad image by saying you have to give up all of your things is very confused or maybe just had a bad experience with minimalism. The point is not to feel deprived, even if you have less than you initially were aiming for you should end up feeling much more content and richer. You end up getting rid of things because you don't really need them, not because you want to live a life of depravation. So when you see people living with just 40 items or something like that and you think "I could never live like that", that's not what this is about. You don't need to live like that unless you don't want to. And they probably love living that way, no harm done.

You need to start asking yourself, what do you want? How do you want your life to be? Because without a roadmap you will end up drifting into your future, rather than taking the wheel of the vehicle of your life, you'd just be a passenger, riding under the mercy of the driver who decides where he takes you.

Create a detailed plan for yourself with achievable deadlines. Now start working towards the life of your dreams. You might have to make sacrifices right now, such as not going out with friends during the weekend so that you can manage your business or side hustle, but in 5 years you will be the owner of an income producing entity, while they stay in exactly the same place they were 5 years ago, going out for drinks on a Friday so that they can compete about whose boss is the worst.

Make sure your goals are measurable and specific so that you can have a way of measuring how you're doing. They should also include a deadline so that you know you need to start putting in the work now if you want to achieve them.

CHAPTER 2: WHY STRIVE FOR LESS

"Simplicity is an acquired taste. Mankind, left free, instinctively complicates life."

- Katharine Fullerton Gerould

Let's face it, this statement is going to go against everything you've been teached so far... Good, most people have lied to us anyway. Who in their right mind would want to strive for less? Before you start to panic we are going to clarify a few things. Obviously this doesn't refer to your work, time you spend with your loved ones or value added to the world. This doesn't mean striving for a worse relationship with your siblings or for a mediocre quality of work. This is aimed towards all of those things that are making your life less enjoyable and impractical.

Strive for less of that which is not adding to your life. If it is not giving you happiness, time, peace, money or anything else that you desire then why are you keeping it? Aim for less of it. Less things laying around your house just for the sake of it, less unused clothes that don't even fit you correctly, less decorations you haven't gotten rid of just because you fear an empty space, less cluttered spaces begging for attention, less stress, less time with your negative coworkers, less late nights working on somebody else's dreams, less health problems, less noise.

Striving for less will give you so much more, more objects you use on a daily basis that make your life simpler, more clothes that you love to wear, more clean spaces that bring you inner peace, more calmness and time to meditate, more time with your family, more money to invest in securing your future.

Again, just because you're a minimalist doesn't mean you have to move to a van and live off $400 per month. Unless you want to do so, if that's your dream then go for it.

Minimalism isn't about being lazy. It is about optimization of resources and living a meaningful life. Cutting out an activity which you're not enjoying or that's not making you productive will free up time that you can use to impact your life positively.

Optimization of resources is a key concept here, since you will be living with less than what you're used to. However you will realize that you don't need much, a powerful concept which will expand to other areas of your life. Imagine if you have to finish a homework for school or university, and you don't have much time because you want to go to the gym and write an article for your blog. Time is a resource which you can optimize, if you only give yourself 4 hours to do something, you can be almost sure it will be completed by the end of those 4 hours, unless it's humanly impossible to do so. There's power in deadlines, use it to your favor.

Most people have never experienced what it is like to have nothing and probably never will. To be honest, neither have I but I have heard stories about people who have (close to) nothing and still manage to be happy and enjoy life. We truly do not need that much in order to survive. And happiness is a state of mind, so why not start being happy right now?

One thing I have learned by being a minimalist is that the less you have, the more value you place in each of your items.

Because they're not just another sweater, it is >the< sweater. You learn to appreciate it by the function it fulfills but also because you value it enough to keep it in your reduced amount of items. If one of your 4 cars breaks down and you send it to the mechanic to get it repaired, you wont miss it as much as you would miss (and need) it if it were your only car. Same goes with pretty much all broadly similar things. The more you have, the more you disconnect from each item.

CHAPTER 3: LESS POSSESSIONS

"The more I threw away, the more I found."

- Don DeLillo

How many items do you own? Can you name all of them? Do you use all of them? Minimalism isn't just about getting rid of stuff but also about keeping it out of your life and making sure it doesn't come crawling back and filling your clean spaces once again.

Each person is different and some tend to collect more things in certain categories, but the more you have, the more likely it is you don't really use everything so it's time to start minimizing your collections. In order to achieve this, you are going to have to search within you. Why do you own so many things from that specific category? Are there any insecurities you're trying to cover or protect by having many items?

Now it is time to start reducing your stuff. There are a few steps which you should go through.

Pick a day in which you'll commit to cleaning your space, whether it is your house or your room. Now pick one specific category in which you'll work on. It can be beauty products, clothes, kitchen utensils, anything. Get everything out and start sorting it. You can either keep the items, discard the items or leave them in an "unsure" pile. The process is pretty simple. Ask yourself if you want to keep it or get rid of it. If you are unsure about an item just put it in a box. If you haven't opened that box in a few months looking for something, just discard it. It is easier to say goodbye to items you want to hold on to if you forget what they are. This means you didn't even need it in the first place, you're just keeping it just in case which is a time that rarely comes.

Get rid of repeated items. Alright, who needs two lemon squeezers, seriously? This might sound like a ridiculous example but everyone has repeated items. And even though I love my lemon squeezer and use it everyday, it would make no sense to have two of them. Do you own any repeated items you could get rid of? Some girls have 3 bottles of foundation. Surely you only need 1 or 2 tops if you use one when you're tanned and the other one during the winter which you should be replacing every now and then anyway, even foundation has an expiration date. Take lipsticks and lipglosses as another example, these usually have a year long lifespan but there are girls who hold on to them for years. Not that they use them but there's no apparent reason to get rid of them, right?

There are items that are necessary for you that might not be useful at all for another person. Let's take a set of brushes and paint as an example. Those might be useful for me as I like to paint as a hobby, but they wouldn't be useful to someone who has no interest in painting and has never painted in his life nor plans to. Where I'm going with this is that only you can decide what it is you need and want to keep. Pay the most attention to the person you are now and not to who you were or who you want to be. If you plan to someday learn how to play the guitar, don't buy a guitar unless you're going to start taking guitar lessons immediately or commit to teach yourself how to play it by watching tutorials on youtube. If there's a difference in who you are and who you want to be, you should aim to be one step closer to who you want to be every single day. However you must also be realist and not buy a whole wardrobe that's like 4 sizes smaller than what you wear at the moment just because you're committed to losing weight. It would be a lot better to leave that shopping for when you hit your target weight and use it as a reward for all your hard work. Also, you can't pretend to buy something for your future self and be 100% sure you're going to like it. As humans we change a lot over time as experiences and years mold us. The person you were 5 years ago isn't the same person you are now, and the future you will also be different. Strive to become better everyday and then if you want to acquire something because it is time to upgrade, use it as a reward for hitting your goal.

I would strongly encourage you to go through the cleaning and discarding process alone so that your decisions won't be biased because of someone who doesn't understand how you live and what you do on a daily basis. Same goes with going shopping, you should avoid doing this with people who encourage you to buy everything you try on and justify buying clothes that don't fit well under some excuse or possible scenario.

Now that you've gone through your stuff and know what it is you need and use often, it is time to organize it in a way in which it also makes sense for your lifestyle. You wouldn't leave shampoo in the living room, right? So figure out a system in which everything you own has a designated space.

Keep items of the same category together or at least those items which make sense to keep relatively close such as shaving cream and a razor or makeup and skin care products.

You decide how you want to organize your stuff and what makes more sense to you. If you usually straighten your hair after you brush your teeth and before applying makeup on, it makes sense to keep all of these things relatively close. While if you like to straighten your hair in the morning while getting ready in your vanity, it makes more sense to keep it there. If you wear shoes inside your house, it makes sense to keep them in your wardrobe with the rest of your clothes but if you put on the shoes before leaving the house, it makes more sense to keep them in a closet near the door.

While you're in the process of reorganizing it is very helpful to figure out your habits and patterns so that you can place your items where they make the most sense and make it easiest for you.

CHAPTER 4: LESS CLOTHES

"I feel like everyday of my life is a funny wardrobe malfunction."

- Nikki Reed

Do you love everything you wear? Are you excited to get up in the morning and get dressed or do you dread having to get up and choose something as you know it'll take you a good 10 minutes because nothing fits and nothing matches? Well, it is time to fix this.

There are countless advantages to owning a minimalist wardrobe, whether it is small in the amount of clothes you own or just very neutral in colors. The amount of time it will save you is life-changing as well as avoiding the frustration in the morning caused by not knowing what to wear. Paralysis by analysis is real, prevent yourself from self-sabotage by culling your wardrobe.

Having a reduced amount of clothes leaves you without much choice so that you have to make a decision faster and sticking to neutral colors makes it easier for you to match the pieces. This doesn't mean all of your clothes have to be grey, black and white but that would also be more efficient.

I'm sure you've seen those posts on social media in which they make fun of billionaires for always wearing the same clothes, however there's a very logical reason why they do this. Famous and successful people including Steve Jobs and Mark

Zuckerberg tend to wear the same outfits quite often. Could it be that people who are this smart wear the same clothes just for the sake of it? Well, not really. As with anything else, people who are this busy have figured out one of the secrets to increased productivity. They dress like this because this is one less decision they have to make that day, therefore making them more efficient when it comes to decision making later on. The more choices you make, the lower your decision making ability becomes as the day goes by.

One of the moments which marked the changing of my wardrobe happened when I was a teenager. I remember when I was younger I went out with a friend of mine and we were just talking about clothes in general. Then he told me about how he used to have like 50 shirts in his closet until he realized he only really wore 5 or 6 of them as they were his favorites. In that moment I realized I did the same, I owned a lot of clothes I didn't even wear or like and they didn't even fit me well enough to be able to argue that they would be useful to me in the future. Some of them I had only gotten because my mom is one of those people who pushes you to buy clothes. That's when I decided to start downsizing on my wardrobe. I basically discarded half of my clothes immediately, I just never wore them. It's amazing how much one word or one sentence can impact your life, that conversation guided me in the direction of a minimalist life without me even realizing it. It also made me obsessed with optimization, specially when it comes to clothes and fashion since I (you might find this surprising) studied image consultancy. So as you can imagine I've always had an interest in fashion and beauty. Yet these are one of the most reduced categories I own and for a good reason.

Interestingly enough, my love for fashion and beauty has only been a motivating factor when becoming a minimalist. You would usually think it would be the other way around and that an image consultant would aim to have the latest fashion trends and a huge collection of makeup. In reality, it taught me to find those products and clothes which fit me best and stick to them. One of the pillars of image is to be true to your style, and my style is minimalist, functional and elegant. How would you describe your style in three words? If you are younger or haven't found your style yet, don't be afraid to experiment, soon you will find the core of your style in those clothes you wear the most and feel the best in.

Even though I'm a minimalist with a considerably reduced wardrobe, I still don't wear the same exact clothes every single day but I'm pretty close to doing so. Although I know my family would riot, they already make fun of me for wearing the same clothes too often. I think they still don't know that I have like 3 shirts that are exactly the same model which I like to wear quite often, so I guess they must think I just live with one shirt and that's it.

One fun thing that happens when you wear the same clothes everyday is that you build a signature look for yourself. I am the girl who is always wearing black. It is my favorite color and it makes me extremely happy to wear only black clothes so I will continue to do so. I've had people say I look like a cartoon character as it appears I never change clothes which I thought was really cool and a powerful branding strategy. I've even had a person offer to introduce me to a guy who also wore only black jeans and a grey shirt, which I thought was hilarious but I kindly declined. So I guess if you wanted to meet someone this would make it easier as your friends would probably introduce you to the minimalists they know.

I'm not saying you need to dress only in black but it helps cut the time you spent matching your outfit in the morning. Same happens with neutral colors but if you're one of those people who enjoys wearing a pop of color in their outfits you can build the core of your wardrobe with neutrals such as beige, white and black and then add something fun to the outfit such as an orange handbag or red trousers. You can have fun while having a minimalist wardrobe.

Now this goes to the ladies, if you need a handbag organization pouch thing it is because you're carrying way too many things on your handbag from which I'm sure you never use even half. Empty your handbag and go through each of the items you're keeping in there, now cut it in half unless you literally have like 5 things. Having a heavy handbag isn't beneficial to your health as it can cause back pain and even a more severe back injury which could end up being permanent. Apart from that, a handbag is something you're always carrying with you. Think about it from the psychological side, your mind is aware there's something you're carrying on your shoulders (back) that's weighting you down. This bag is stopping you from going faster and being/feeling free. Do not let your handbag or bag become a burden, it is supposed to be a very useful item that can help you carry the tools you need in order to perform at a top level.

I only bring what's necessary and I can find any item by just opening my handbag. You really don't need that much, specially if you're only going to run some errands or go to a few classes. If you need to, make a list of the items you need on a daily basis and those which are essentials that you use quite often such as tissues, hand sanitizer or a pen.

Now it's time to go through your closet. I dare you to do the capsule wardrobe for at least a month. You probably wear roughly the same clothes everyday anyway. I mean, you must have a favorite shirt, pair of pants and shoes. Imagine wearing those more often and having more items in your wardrobe which you enjoy almost as much. Plus, you don't have to continue doing this afterwards if you don't want to. It's only an experiment.

When doing a capsule wardrobe a lot of people like having different items as it will give them a lot more looks. You could create up to like 500 look combinations if you really try to optimize your pieces. Whether you get bored wearing the same thing everyday and prefer to take this approach or don't mind to have like 4 total outfit combinations is up to you. But going through this experience will definitely teach you a lot, even if you decide not to stick to having a capsule wardrobe after the season is over.

There are a few basics to follow when building a capsule wardrobe to make it a lot easier. Stick to mostly neutral colors. Have a color palette consisting of three neutral colors (black, white, blue) and two accent colors (red, green). Take the season you're in in consideration so that you can have appropriate clothes for the weather. Have your capsule wardrobe be flexible enough to be able to go to work or a formal event as well as just spend a relaxing evening in your home. Build it around a few essential items such as a jacket, a few shirts, jeans or leggings and comfortable shoes. Document your process and feelings, you might discover something you weren't aware of once you're separated from your excess clothes. Make it fun, upload pictures to instagram or write about it and publish it.

Okay, time to go through your stuff. There are a few guidelines to follow if you want to make getting rid of stuff easier. If it is broken, is falling apart or has a hole, throw it away. If you haven't worn it in over a year, throw it away. If it is an item you have to alter or fix but haven't brought yourself to do so, get rid of it unless you commit to getting it altered in the next 3 days. If it looks old in a bad way or outdated, get rid of it. If you don't like it, put it in the donating pile. If it does not fit you, throw it away. This applies if it is too big, too small or if the color or design just don't go well with you.

Once you've gone through all your stuff and donated the clothes you haven't used in a year that you keep telling yourself you will wear but never do it is time to address the problem of how they got into your closet in the first place. Because the only one who could've put those clothes there is you. There's no excuse because even if someone pressured you to buy a certain item, it was you who ultimately had to say yes, take it home and place it in your closet.

Why are you buying clothes you don't wear and you know you're not going to wear? Is it because you go shopping with someone who pushes you to buy stuff? Or do you convince yourself to buy it for whatever reason? Well, whatever it is, it is time to stop. There are some simple tricks to use if you want to make sure you really want to make the purchase.

Wait 24 hours before getting it. You can go into the store, try it on, carry it around, but you have to wait 24 hours before you buy it. If you didn't like it enough to go back to the store just to get it then it's probably because you don't like it enough in the first place. This technique will also stop you from buying things on impulse, specially if they're on sale. If you're buying online you can look at it and even save it but then again, do not buy it until 24 hours have gone by. Which brings me to the next tip.

Ask yourself if you would buy it if it was twice or even 10 times the price it currently is. Buying an item just because it is on sale is a huge mistake. You'll start rationalizing why you should get it just because of the price. You've been a victim of marketing.

Ask yourself if you would replace an item you currently own for this piece. I understand we sometimes need to replace an item because it's time to do so. I currently need to buy new black leggings as mine are getting to the end of their life period, they've been through enough. However, if you had new black leggings and wanted to acquire a new pair, would you replace them for this one? Imagine you were doing a capsule wardrobe, would you replace your jeans to get them in the capsule?

Ask yourself if you need them or if you just want them. Most of the things we want to buy we don't actually need. It's different if you want to buy a coat because it's 6 degrees Celsius than wanting to buy it because it's on sale.

If you've passed all of these questions there is one final topic to take into consideration. Is this going to last? We all know those fashion brands that seem to make clothes that will only last 2 wears and then fall apart in the washing machine. If you think about it, these end up being more expensive than if you chose a higher quality product that's going to last you for years. Think of cost per wear. Is this item going to cost you $10 per wear or $0.10? If you buy a $30 handbag and use it 3 times before throwing it away or giving it to someone, that handbag costed you $10 per wear. If you buy a designer bag for $300 and wear it everyday for a year, that handbag costed you $0.82 cents per wear. And since it's designer it's probably well made and will last you at least for another two years of constant use.

Also, avoid temptation. Do not watch haul videos on the Internet if they tempt you to buy stuff. Try to avoid them until you're no longer susceptible to them.

Whatever it is you decide to do with your wardrobe, remember to listen to your style. Don't follow trends just because they're everywhere, follow your true style and you'll always have a wardrobe which you love. Doesn't matter if you have 15 items or 92.

CHAPTER 5: LESS DECORATION

"Minimalism is the pursuit of the essence of things, not the appearance."

- Claudio Silvestrin

As we have seen in previous chapters, minimalism is about having enough. This applies to decoration as well. Even having decoration for the sake of it is a little bit counterintuitive if we're aiming towards a minimalist lifestyle.

There's nothing inherently wrong about decoration. It could even result inspiring to you if you know how to choose it right. Hanging inspiring pictures from your mentors or people you admire will drive you to be better. Creating a vision board with every goal you want to accomplish is also a good idea, don't forget to be as specific as you can with your goals and use pictures that represent them well.

Just as there is good decoration, there are other types of decoration which might be distracting you from your goals. Does it ever happen to you that you're about to do something and then forget because something else caught your attention? This could even be clutter or another activity which you need to do that you left in plain sight. Well, modify your space and keep it as clean as possible so that there's nothing distracting you from carrying out the most important task of the day.

When you do get furniture, get furniture that you will enjoy using and don't treat it just like decoration. I'm including it in this chapter because it is what you'll most likely seeing the most out of all the other categories. Furniture is supposed to be used and enjoyed. It should be comfortable, useful and invite you to use it. It isn't enough for a couch to just look beautiful, what's the point of having a couch if you don't even want to sit on it? Also, do yourself a favor and don't choose a color such as white or beige for a sofa. Accidents do happen. I probably shouldn't be telling you this as my family will most likely read this book but I once spilled wine on my mom's white sofa while she was away. Sorry mom! But even drinking coffee or tea feels like a dangerous activity in that couch.

When decorating a room you should take a few factors into consideration.

Color scheme: just like with your closet, your spaces should also have some sort of color palette that unifies the room and makes it make sense. Just because you're a minimalist doesn't mean you have to own only black, white and grey furniture but it is a good idea to stick to neutrals when it comes to big pieces of decoration such as the painting of a wall or the color of the couch since these are a lot harder to change than a painting or a pillow. If you want to add touches of color you can do so by adding little statement pieces throughout the space that will make it come alive without it being overwhelming.

Coherency: Would it make sense to have the oven in the living room? This might be a little bit of an extreme example but it illustrates the point. Your items should be placed according to their use and where it makes more sense to keep them. Just like you wouldn't keep spoons in the bathroom you shouldn't have your clothes laying around the house.

Harmony: This has to do with the color scheme but mostly with how the pieces themselves go together. You need to aim to decorate in a way in which the pieces in your spaces go well with each other and help the other ones look better instead of hiding them. Even if you're hanging artwork on the walls you should aim to make it go with the overall vibes of the room. You can notice perfect harmony in a room in which all the pieces go together and enhance the others rather than stealing attention from them.

Quality: make sure to look for quality items while decorating any room, furniture is one of those things which will most likely stay with you for a few years and you want it to last. They are also going to be more expensive than just buying a shirt so it's not like you can just buy a couch and if you don't like it then bury it somewhere, because 1 you probably paid a lot for it, 2 it is massive and 3 that would just be extremely wasteful.

If you live with other people make sure to talk to them about the changes in the decoration and what their thoughts are if they want to participate in the decorating or a common room. If you have a joint bank account also ask them before making a big purchase because it is their money as well.

CHAPTER 6: LESS DEBT

―――――――――

"Too many people spend money they haven't earned, to buy things they don't want, to impress people they don't like."

- Will Rogers

―――――――――

Debt refers to the amount of money you owe to other people or to the bank. This means that even if you are currently in possession of that money, it is not really yours as you will have to pay it back to its owner or the bank.

When it comes to debt, there are two types of debt: good debt and bad debt. We are going to focus on the bad debt on this book as it is what we want to reduce. If you would like to know more about good debt it will be included in another book so stay tuned for future publications.

One interesting concept that not many people understand is that when you finance an item with debt (this can be a house, a car or even a phone or computer), this item isn't yours until you finish paying it. Have you taken the time to read the fine print? The item itself is the collateral to your debt, which is why when you can't pay the mortgage the bank can take away your house and then resell it. It wasn't really yours yet! It becomes yours once you make the final payment.

I was talking to a lawyer a few days ago about this topic and he was explaining that even when you get a contract for your phone at a telecommunications company and they give you a new iPhone or whatever, the company legally owns that phone it until you've finished paying it. Talk about fine print! This is why when you have a 24 month phone contract you have to pay a fine if you decide to end it before that time frame. They're not charging you the cancellation of the service itself, they're charging you what's left to pay of the phone.

Debt is fun until you have to pay it back, this is why a lot of people get credit cards and then spend until they reach the card's limit. The best path if you're not in debt and don't have to get into debt for a good and urgent reason is to stay out of it. And if you're going to get a credit card only get it if you are sure you can pay off the balance at the end of the month. Make sure the interest rate is manageable as well, some credit card companies charge 30% in interest rates.

If you're not in debt, work towards creating an emergency fund. According to Bankrate, 61% of Americans can't afford a $1,000 emergency. Your emergency fund should be at least $1,000. Once you have enough in your emergency fund, works towards saving 6 months worth of expenses. If anything happens and you lose your main source of income, you will be covered for a few months until you figure out what to do and get a new job or build another source of income. There's nothing worse than being extremely in need of money and not being able to access it. People become desperate and resort to irrational actions to get the money they need to make it through the month. These can end up in illegal activities such as robbing other people or even selling illegal substances.

Understandably, there are moments in which we need to use debt such as in the case of an emergency. This happens when we haven't prepared correctly to absorb such cost and it can cause us to end up paying a lot more in interests in the long run than if we had saved at least $1,000 in case of an emergency and use that to cover it and then use debt to cover the rest. What makes going into debt so expensive are the interests as you end up not paying only the $5,000 you borrowed but also a percentage on top of that, which could end up making the final payment something like $6,500. There are a few bits of information to take into consideration if you plan to get a credit card or loan. Before getting a credit card make sure you can pay the balance every month. Find out how much the interest rate is and set reminders to pay the monthly balance on time.

While we're in the topic of debt, you shouldn't get into debt to fund your living expenses. This will only put you in a whole that becomes deeper each month. Your expenses should be 80% of your income at the most. If you're living above what you can afford, you will soon be in debt plus there's no room for errors such as losing your job or going through a financial crisis. Which let's be real, can happen at any moment and it is best to be prepared for it than to be taken by surprise. Take care of yourself and live below your means. Your monthly income should allow you to live decently and save up some money each month.

Minimalism can and will most likely help you reduce your monthly expenses. If you don't know where to start, start going through your subscriptions and unsubscribe from all of those which you're not using. Even those $25 per month from subscriptions can make a difference, specially if you look at it over time. If you have a gym membership and you haven't been to the gym in two months (which being realistic it's more like 6 months), you're just throwing away money. That's extremely wasteful, think about what you could be doing with

$40 extra per month or $400 per year, assuming you only went two months like most people do. Be honest with yourself and cancel that membership, maybe it is time to try other sports such as tennis or basketball until you find one that you enjoy.

If you are currently in debt and need to pay it off, it is essential that you find a way to do so every month and tackle it as soon as possible if you can. Some financial gurus suggest you use a technique called the snowball effect. In which you focus on paying off smaller debts (even if they have a lower interest) so that you feel accomplished and that motivates you to take on bigger and more expensive debts and you use the payments from those smaller loans now towards the bigger ones in order to pay a bigger amount per month. You can also pay off the highest interest debt first as that's the one that grows the most each month. Whatever method you choose is up to you and what you find works better with your personality and thought process, aim towards being debt free.

Also, remember someone lended you that money, how would you feel if you lended someone $1,000 and they didn't pay it back? The best is just to pay it off and learn the lesson in order to not make the same mistake of falling into a horrible debt again.

CHAPTER 7: MORE MONEY

"It's not your salary that makes you rich, it's your spending habits."

- Charles A. Jaffe

How do you make money as a minimalist is an easy question to answer. Making money is such a huge topic because usually it is your job which takes the most amount of your time. In order to leave your job you would either need to 1 reduce your expenses or 2 increase your income. You could also create your own sources of income to live comfortably without having to worry about having a job and performing well in it. Minimalism helps free your time, even if it is your free time after work. Time which you can make productive by creating a second source of income which could eventually end up being the main one.

All my life I knew I wanted to be an entrepreneur and I can gladly say it is a lot easier to do it now than it was 10 years ago thanks to new technologies and systems that have been implemented over time. My favorite ones of course are the ones related to amazon because I believe they resonate with me and what I want to do but even if those business models are not of your interest there are many options left. Here are some ways in which you can create a second or even third income source.

Write a book.
One of the ways to make passive income while doing

something you enjoy is to write a book. If you enjoy writing, like me, this won't feel tedious even if you're writing 4,000 per day as a way to challenge yourself. Which brings me to the second way to make passive income online.

Start a blog.
Blogs can be an amazing way to connect with people with the same interests as you. If you decide to write about a topic which you're passionate about such as minimalism, your blog will most likely attract the attention of minimalists if you're creating value for them in the form of entertainment or education. This would cost around $120 for both the domain and the hosting and then you would have to produce the content yourself or hire a ghostwriter. There are plenty of websites that you can use to do this such as fiverr or upwork.

Amazon FBA
You've probably seen people making a ton of money off of amazon FBA. Aim to fulfill a need in a market that's not too saturated. Even though the investment needed to start selling on amazon FBA is not as high as the investment needed to start other businesses, it is still considerably higher than starting a blog or with amazon KDP.

Start a YouTube channel
Another way of making money online is to start a YouTube channel. There are people who are better at talking than they are at writing and vice versa. The best part about starting a YouTube channel is that the abilities needed aren't that many but you will need video editing and speaking skills and you can even film the videos with your phone, virtually anywhere in the world. You can use editing programs which basically come with your computer or invest in a professional editing software. The cost to start with YouTube is virtually zero as you can start using what you already own. The highest cost would be the time you'll need to invest in learning how to edit a video so that you can upload a better version and also learn how to make thumbnails that catch the viewer's attention.

Freelance websites
Such as Fiverr or Upwork let you share your talents with the world and the customers hire you as a freelancer. While this is not passive income, you can use it to build your savings or to fund your passive income investments.

One of the topics that most people living outside the US worry about is how they're going to receive a payment. I know this because it happened to me. The cheque system is inefficient because it takes a long time to get said cheque if your country's postal service isn't fast and if you live far away it takes a long time for the package to travel until it gets to you.

Don't worry if you don't live inside the US as there's this payment method called Payoneer. You can apply for an American bank account online by giving the details of your local bank account and use it to receive payments from amazon, google or other platforms. You can go to their website or create your account using this link:

**https://share.payoneer.com/nav/
7UNFJe5DbiEonWEafiTiBFRIUyH2iSp21BVulrJzTZlX4z6dm
ELA7jARGGsoM6oyKl- pYbdtmvz3A6aZY3vtQ2**

If you use the link to create your account you and me both get $25, plus you can get another $25 if you refer the service to a friend by using your own share code.

There's one important thing about making more money and it is that just because you're making more money doesn't mean you should spend more, it is a lot more sensible to invest this money and keep living how you're living at the moment until you can afford to live any life you want because of how you built your investment portfolio. If you want 5 cars, go ahead and get your 5 cars, just make sure to buy them with the income you get from your investments rather than the income you make by working a job because then, you're paying for the cars with your time rather than with your value.

Think of every new dollar you acquire as someone who works for you to make you more money. If you spend that dollar then you're not receiving that benefit but if you invest it, all the extra money that dollar is making will go directly back to you.

If you want to become rich or even live a comfortable life it is essential that you change your beliefs about money. Money isn't good or bad, it depends on what you do with it that determines its effect on your life. It is easier to aim to have a lot of money so that you end up living comfortably later in life than aim to live comfortably and then struggling because you can't make ends meet. One of the most frustrating and stressful situations you can get yourself into is the position in which you can't even afford to pay for rent or food. It is better to have too much money than too little money, plus you can always donate the money you don't want or feel like you don't need.

It is also important to change your belief that there's a scarcity of money, just because you're making money doesn't mean someone else's money is being taken. When you create value you're basically creating money (not really, but stick with me). When you build a house in a previously empty space, you're creating value because otherwise that space wasn't being productive. Even if you spend money on materials and labor it's not like you're throwing that money away because you're getting a house in return and those people are getting paid for their work and the company from which you acquire the materials from are getting paid for supplying a good that's in demand and that money is probably also going towards the people working at the company who help run it. In the end, you get to enjoy a beautiful house to live in and create wonderful memories and everyone else gets paid based on the value they added to the house. Now even the properties next to your house raised their value thanks to your contribution. Then when you want to move you can sell the house and get back probably even more than what it costed you to build it. There is no such thing as a shortage of money if you know how to create value.

CHAPTER 8: MINIMALIST BUDGET

"I make myself rich by making my wants few."

- Henry David Thoreau

Budgeting might not be your favorite activity but it is one of the most important things you can dedicate time and attention to. Knowing where your money is going will make your priorities clearer as well as help you identify the reason why there's no money left in your bank account at the end of the month. Mysterious, right?

Budgets are basically divided in two parts, income and expenses. Income is what's coming in every month, here is where your salary and other income sources are located. Expenses are what's going out every month such as rent and car payments. In order for you to have an accurate idea of what's going on with your money, you should have a budget with separated categories that include the essentials but also makes it easy to see where your money is going and why.

INCOME

The best way to live a better life with more freedom is to increase your income. You can do this in many different ways. The traditional one is to increase your abilities so that you will be paid more by going up in the job you currently have. Another one is to do a side job on top of your normal job.

Starting a business on your free time or investing in assets so that they will generate income for you every month. Out of all the options you have to increase your income, increasing your assets is the one which will give you freedom because it doesn't depend on time in the long run. If you work at a job, you're being paid for your time which means that if you're not working you're not being paid, while if you have passive income streams, you're being paid even when you're asleep because you already put in the work to generate that stream.

EXPENSES

Expenses should be lower than your income so that you have the chance to use the extra in investments or save it. Even when your income goes up, your expenses shouldn't go up with it in the same proportion. The famous "live below your means" advice is one of the best you can get in the finance topic because many people go into debt just to finance a luxurious lifestyle they didn't even earn in the first place. If your income is low you can reduce your expenses but it is a lot more fun to increase your income instead. Most minimalists end up reducing their expenses because they realize that what they thought they needed isn't really necessary. So as part of the exercises in this book, I would suggest you look at your monthly expenses with your full attention and reduce those which you don't need or that aren't adding to your dream life.

When it comes to money, there are other ways to make money as well as other types of expenses than the ones we are used to. Assets refer to the things that are making us money without us having to work per se, trading time for money.

ASSETS

Increase your assets to have new sources of income coming into your account every month without you having to spend your time in them. Examples such as ebooks or a Youtube channel in which you have to make a high time or money investment at the start but then generate income every month passively are examples of this as well as rental properties or intellectual property. The type of assets you want to acquire is up to you and they'll depend on your own risk tolerance and how much time and money you're able to invest at the time.

LIABILITIES

Decrease your liabilities, these are the things that are taking money away from you each month and that are usually for a long period of time so you can't really change them such as a debt, car loan or a mortgage.

There are some misconceptions people have which might sound like a shock to you because they go against everything we've been taught

A house is a liability, not an investment. Think about it, a house takes money away from you every single month without producing anything (unless you are renting part of it on airbnb or other sites). This can't be classified as an investment, so it's a liability because you have to pay for it every month, not the other way around. Even after you've finished paying for it you still have to pay for other costs such as maintenance and reparations. An investment property is very different, this is a property which is meant to be rented as much time as possible so that it continues to generate income. If you rent your house for a year, even when you have to pay for some reparations costs and a mortgage, you have an asset. If you have a house with 5 rooms and you only use 2 and rent the other 3 then that's an asset because that rental will most likely pay for the house and you end up living there for "free".

Same scenario happens with a car, if you buy your car on credit it is something that will continue to take money away from your bank account and therefore is classified as a liability. Now let's say you own a car rental company, each car will generate you income when it is being used by another person who rents that car, in this case each car is an asset.

Part of the importance of this chapter is because I want you to live the best life possible and to be able to spend your time how you want it and doing something meaningful such as spending it with your family or working at something which actually fulfills you. Money itself isn't the goal, but the freedom it brings and the ability to help others with it.

Now that we have gone through all of the definitions it is time to make your own budget and include your income, expenses, assets and liabilities. You can do this on an excel sheet, just make sure you include everything so that you can identify where your money is going and where it is coming from. Another way to identify where your money is going is to look at your card statement, in here you can see the place you spent money in, the date and the amount.

You can do two or even three different excel sheets, one for the real scenario in which you are at the moment and then another with your dream income statement in which you include many assets and increased income but also in what you want to spend your money such as travel or courses in which you learn valuable information.

Once you finish this exercise you will end up feeling one of two ways, "Wow, I'm actually doing pretty well" or "Wow, I should really change my spending habits." Whatever it is you end up with, work to be better than the day before.

CHAPTER 9: LESS CLUTTER

"Look around. All that clutter used to be money."

- Unknown

Okay, real talk. Why are you even keeping stuff that you have already categorized as clutter still unorganized and inside your home? I can assure you that the moment you read the word clutter you had already formed an idea in your mind of the items or areas within your house that fall under this definition. You're probably like: oh yeah I need to get rid of that and organize my bedside table.

No one needs clutter in their life. The name itself tells the whole story, "clutter". It is not needed or wanted and minimalism helps massively to keep this away for good.

Going back to the topic of decoration and how it distracted us, clutter is even more distracting. The worst part is that we use organizing as an activity to help us avoid important tasks which we need to complete but end up procrastinating on. It happened to me that the day before the calculus midterm I suddenly became fixed on cleaning my desk. If it had already been clean and organized then I would've had no excuse to not study and would've probably spent a lot more time studying and probably getting better grades.

I remember watching a few videos on organization a few years ago and I was just impressed by how many things those people owned. Videos such as "how I organize my makeup collection" already imply that said collection is massive and that it needs organizing. My makeup "collection" is 11 items, even if I tried to organize it, it would just be one compartment per item. It might sound like a ridiculously small makeup collection but the truth is, I don't need more and even if I had more items I wouldn't use them so it wouldn't make sense to buy more.

If you decide you want to have many items (which I doubt is the case as this is a book on minimalism) then that could go one of two ways, the first one is that you keep it organized and dedicate a considerable amount of time to making sure it is always either kept organized or organizing. The other scenario is that you get lazy or just busy and can't organize for a few days or weeks and it ends up being a mess. Either way, it doesn't sound very promising.

Part of the key of reducing clutter and probably even eliminate it from your life for good is just to own fewer items. Think about it, we all have that chair or sofa in our bed which is "the chair". You know which one I'm talking about, the one we put the clothes that have been used but aren't dirty yet. If unsupervised, this chair ends up becoming a mountain of clothes, hiding the chair almost entirely. Now, what happens if you decided to adopt the capsule wardrobe trend for that season? Even if you were using the chair as a place to keep some of your clothes, chances are there aren't even enough items for a clothes mountain to form on top of it. I know this isn't the solution to the problem itself, but it does make it more manageable. The advantage of it being more manageable is that you can form habits that will help with this problem and you will see results right away as the pile to go through is now just 2 pairs of pants and a shirt.

If you need a good guide to declutter, I suggest you first go through all of your stuff, it doesn't matter if you're thinking about decluttering it or not it is always important to have a good idea of everything you own.

The steps in decluttering your house are very similar to the steps in decluttering your wardrobe, except you don't try on these items of course.

First you need to get out everything you own that's in the same "category" so if you're planning on decluttering your kitchen you might want to start with utensils such as forks and knives but don't just stop there, get out all the other small items that would classify as utensils such as a bottle opener and a lemon squeezer and ask yourself with each and every item if you actually use them or if you plan on using them soon. It is important not to lie to yourself and saying you will use something that still has the tag on, because you're very unlikely to end up using it and it would better serve another person. If you decide to get it out of your cupboard, you can give it to your friend who loves to cook and bake or you can donate it so that another person can use it. If you have items that you're unsure about you can keep them in a sealed box, out of sight. with time you will most likely forget about them and then you can donate the box if you don't open it for a while. However if you do open it searching for something you left in there, that means that's a useful item worth keeping.

Now, clutter not only refers to items, it can also be applied to relationships and habits. If you dedicate a lot of time to a toxic relationship it's still going to do you more bad than good and even lower the quality of your life. Choose well who you want to spend time with and also pick the activities you want to do rather than those you feel obligated to do even when they're not useful. It is better to have fewer but meaningful connections with people you enjoy spending time with who are aligned with you in their values and interests.

CHAPTER 10: LESS STRESS

"Make things as simple as possible but no simpler."

- Albert Einstein

Stress is the literal silent killer. We don't realize how much stress affects us and our daily life until we look back and notice the damage.

I was considering to include this within the health chapter but I figured it deserved a whole chapter. A whole lot of people suffer from stress and they don't even know it, which is a huge problem.

Stress can cause your hair to fall, your digestive system to not function correctly and other health complications. It also kills neurons if it is intense and prolonged. Yes, it can hurt your brain if you don't watch it.

There are several ways you can reduce stress but they will require you to consciously work on using them.

Stop procrastinating: It is usually those things that need to be done the most the ones we end up procrastinating in. Stop putting these off, it will only lead to more stress and a reduced time frame for you to get it done.

Exercise: It is no secret that exercising relaxes you, it also has a lot of benefits for your health and brain. Plus, it makes you feel amazing because it releases endorphins. Exercising often will also make you feel accomplished when you start seeing the results of your hard work.

Meditation: It has been scientifically proven that meditation helps you calm down and increase your mindfulness. Simply put, when you're meditating you can either do it to resolve a problem, relax or just for contemplation. If you're using meditation to solve a problem, what happens is that you concentrate on that problem until you find solutions or a way to proceed. While you're thinking about this problem in particular, all the noise from other problems or thoughts will be moved to the background so that you can concentrate. If you're meditating to relax, try thinking about something that brings you joy. I like to think I'm just walking in a field.

It makes no sense to stress about things that aren't going to happen or that are unlikely to happen. Which means you shouldn't be living in the future, obsessing about how things are going to be in a few years. Living in the future causes anxiety. This doesn't mean you should be living in the past either as that causes depression. Aim to live in the moment and enjoy the experiences you're going through. And even if you're going through a bad moment you can be certain that it will pass, and that too will come to an end.

Try to remove yourself from situations which stress you without any good reason. This is different for each person but you can easily identify which ones they are. What do you avoid the most doing? For me it was very stressful to go into the weights area of the gym but I tried not to give it much thought as that only made it worse and just go in. Now it almost feels natural and I realized it was an unjustified fear.

If social media stresses you because you're looking at everything everyone else has then it would be sensible to change the people you're following or to reduce your usage of social media. If you're using it for business then you can keep uploading and managing your profiles or have someone else do it for you. The goal is to reduce the time you spend in stressful situations or to try to avoid them as much as possible.

CHAPTER 11: JUST ENOUGH

―――――――――――――――――

"Nothing is enough for the man to whom enough is too little."

- Epicurus

―――――――――――――――――

If you had to reduce everything you own to just a few items, what would you keep? If you had to live one year with just these items, which ones would you choose?

If you've watched some minimalism videos on Youtube you might have come across some that are titled something like: everything I own. And it's like 40 items. I personally couldn't own just 40 items but I find it cool that they can, however it's just not my cup of tea.

The concept of just enough is a bit tricky as it varies from person to person but making a list of essentials is a great help if you want to figure out what is it that really matters to you. If you don't remember most of your items it's probably because you don't use them so make it a goal for yourself to live with only those items which you actually use rather than holding on to a lot of stuff that doesn't add to your life or the overall happiness.

Try making a detailed list of everything you own, even if it's just for fun. It will teach you which items you actually value the most. You can also make a list of all your essentials and which ones you would take if you were backpacking through the world for a year. This is going to be an example of a list which you can use as some sort of template for your items when you're going to travel.

If you want to make it even more interesting, try reducing the list in half. This second list will give you the core essentials. Remember this is just a simulation of a scenario, the chances that you'll have to live only with those items are minimal. But if you ever want to travel light you can just take a look at this list to find out what you considered essential. One interesting hack is that you can pretty much live for months with just the items that you would use on a two week period. So even if you're going traveling for a year, packing for two weeks should be enough unless the climate changes considerably between the places you're visiting. Of course items like shampoo and toothpaste aren't included here but almost every other item goes by this rule.

Finding the ideal amount of just enough items depends on each person because only you can know how much you need. This amount will also change depending on your age and the moment of your life that you're going through.

CHAPTER 12: WHAT REAL WEALTH LOOKS LIKE

"Our souls are not hungry for fame, comfort, wealth or power.
Our souls are hungry for meaning, for the sense that we have
figured out how to live so that our lives matter."

- Harold Kushner

Regardless of the number in your bank account, can you say
you're a wealthy person? Do you have a family that loves you,
meaningful relationships with friends, and spend your day
doing things you love to do or dedicating time to a cause you
believe in?

Or do you spend your day surrounded by people who mean
nothing to you, far away from your family, trying to impress the
neighbors and working at a job that's slowly killing your soul
only to come home too tired to even spend time with the
people who waited all day to see you?

For me, there are 5 classifications of wealth. Apart from the
obvious one which is monetary wealth, there's time wealth,
peace wealth, family and relationships and freedom.

Monetary wealth is simple: having enough money to cover
your necessities each month such as rent and food, being able
to save a percentage of your income without feeling deprived
of that money and a bit extra to spend in something you want
such as a trip to New York or even a new computer. This type
of wealth means nothing if you do not have the other types of
wealth as well.

Time wealth is not spending more time with your coworkers than you spend with your spouse and children. It is not having to wake up at 5 am just because you have to go to work at a company you don't even like. You are free to spend time with those you love when you want to do so. You are able to work when you feel inspired or during the designated time you set yourself. Time wealth is being the owner of your time, not following the schedule someone else made for you.

Peace wealth is not having to stress about having to pay the bills as you know exactly how much they're going to be and you're prepared and happy to pay them as they make your life more enjoyable. It doesn't matter if your rent is $600 or $4,000 per month, if you're stressing about not being able to pay it then you're not living a life of wealth. Because you can't enjoy your life even if you're living in a mansion. You also live a life in which you follow your values and stick to them when it's time to make any decisions. Things change, people change, situations change but your values should stay the same. If it is against the law, it's not worth it. You're not worrying about the FBI showing at your company looking for you. You can go to sleep at night without stressing about paying the bills or being arrested, you have peace.

You have also established meaningful relationships which you keep nurturing every day with people who love you for you. You are wealthy in love. Human beings are social beings, we need to interact with others in order to feel like we belong. Family is one of the most important things in your life. Even if your blood family is small or are no longer with you, there are people who become so close to you that they become family. Sometimes the bonds we make are even stronger than those bonds made by blood. Love and protect your family and nurture those relationships which are important to you.

Freedom. You can do whatever you want, whenever you want and get anything you want when you want it. You travel to Ethiopia and become aware of the poverty of the country so you decide to start a school because you believe education is the first step to get out of poverty. You have freedom to pursue your dreams, travel anywhere you want and help all of those causes that touch your heart. Freedom wealth consists of a mix of monetary wealth and time wealth but there's also a psychological side to it. Most people create their own cages without even realizing it, which restrains the way they live their lives. Freedom also includes not worrying about what other people are going to say. It is your life after all and you are the one who has to live it, so why not make it as enjoyable as possible?

There's one simple question which will help you find out if you're living the life you want or the life someone else chose for you. If you had the chance to do whatever it is you wanted in life, would you be doing what you're doing right now? I know I would, at least for the most part.

If your answer to that question was anything less than yes, it is time to make some serious changes in your life. I know it is hard to decide to take that first step but it is worth it. The change might not be immediate but when you look back in a few years you'll thank yourself for taking the decision to make a change and then working towards building the life of your dreams.

I must confess that through the years I failed to look for the others classifications of wealth while I was busy searching for money. It isn't until you realize that even money isn't as valuable as the other types of wealth that you focus on building a life which is rich in all classifications of wealth. What's the point of being a millionaire if you can't even enjoy it if you:

a)   Lack the time to even spend a nice relaxing evening at the home of your dreams.

b)   Can't sleep at night since you feel someone is coming to get you because the way you acquired your wealth wasn't ethical or legal.

c)   Your family hates you because you don't even spend time with them as you're so busy. They don't even know who you are anymore.

d)   Can't afford to take a vacation because everyone needs you at your work for it to continue running smoothly.

It is just not worth it, and it is true what they say: more money, more problems. Save yourself from the problems by making sure you're doing things right from the start. What we want to achieve is your freedom, freedom from stuff and other constraints so that you can do what you enjoy and own what's useful.

Of course, money will be a great help in achieving other goals, it is a lot easier to start a business if you have the starting capital or take a course on the topic before you start so that you shorten your learning curve. So, don't take money as the goal. The goal is freedom, money is the tool which will help you get there a lot faster.

CHAPTER 13: EXPERIENCES

———————————————

"Create space and time to listen to your heart and soul. Then you'll know what matters the most."

-from bemorewithless.com

———————————————

What's going to last you more than a pair of new shoes? An experience. Experiences last a lifetime and no one can take them away from you because they become part of who you are and it shapes the person you become. So unless you have really bad memory or something happens they will remain with you. Aim to become a collector of experiences rather than a collector of items. They also add to your knowledge and give you a new perspective. If you travel I can assure you that you'll go back to your country with at least one idea for a business or a book.

This happened to me, I hadn't realized what percentage of the population is above 65 years old in Spain, mostly because you're used to seeing numbers but aren't aware of how those numbers translate to how people live and the kind of businesses that flourish in these special situations. Thinking about the future, I came back to this country with a business idea similar to the ones that were flourishing there since we, too have an aging population. Thanks to globalization, most of the world is pretty much similar in the values that we share, however laws, language and lifestyle are other topics which are important to take into consideration when traveling to a country that's so different to ours. What is legal in this country might not be legal in other countries, this is something you should look at when you're traveling to a country that's different to yours and in which you don't speak the language because it might be a lot harder to reach an agreement or to correct a misunderstanding when you don't understand others. Even though I don't expect you to know and speak the language of every single country you visit, it would be a good idea to learn at least a few phrases in said language and important but simple concepts such as big, small, fast, slow, stop, continue, etc. As well as useful words such as hungry, food, cold, hot, bathroom, etc. Even speaking like a caveman is preferable than not being understood at all, plus there are apps which translate text and audio in a matter of seconds if you needed to understand something or speak to someone urgently.

Every city holds a treasure that becomes available for those who visit and the most beautiful part of this is that no one will have the same experience as you. We are all unique and have different perspectives and thought processes. When you purchase a bag from one brand and another person purchases the same bag, you end up having exactly the same product. Whether you want to personalize it in some way or not is up to you but it is essentially the same bag. When you travel somewhere you've never been before, the experience you have there will be extremely different from the experience other travelers have. And even more different than the experience and memories someone who lives there has. Even if you're having a drink together, your experiences will be different since he might be thinking about the time he went there for his birthday or might be thinking about coming back next week, when you're on your way back to your home city.

When was the last time you traveled outside the country? What about inside the country? What about somewhere near that you've never been to? Experiences not only have to be traveling ones, they can also happen in the park near your house. There's no excuse for not even visiting a new place that's near where you live, unless you don't like it for some reason. Traveling is important as it broadens your horizons and represents a way of learning by experiencing the new cultures, sights, smells and textures. It also doesn't require you to spend a lot of money as there are activities and day tours you can do for free. Join a free club or fitness class and meet new people. Everyone has something to teach us if we are willing to learn.

Even something as simple as going out to eat by yourself to a restaurant you enjoy can be an experience. However, the catch is that you're not allowed to use your phone or any other electronic device. We've gotten too used to being "with someone" even if this someone is a person we are talking to on Whatsapp. Also, do not take a book with you as that will distract you. You may have noticed that time flies when you're reading, this is because your mind is occupied with an activity so it concentrates on the story you're reading. The goal is that you spend time with the most important person, yourself. When was the last time you talked to yourself and evaluated your feelings and thoughts on a deeper level? Minimalism, since it reduces the noise around you, will make you get to know yourself better. Learn how to be alone with your thoughts and appreciate them as they could reveal patterns or feelings you weren't aware of but that might be affecting your life. If you want you can take a notebook and a pen to write any thoughts or ideas you have while you're enjoying dinner.

Who knows, you might even end up writing a short story or the start of the book you've been postponing.

The moment in which I spend more time with my thoughts (if you could say so) is when I'm about to go to bed. Every time I'm laying in the dark I start thinking, which becomes quite problematic as sleep is extremely important for productivity and overall body functions. The interesting part of this story is that I usually get my best ideas or fastest writing at this time. If what I plan to write is extensive, I get out my phone or computer to have it ready to switch to a document. I get extremely creative at night (at around 10 pm or later) and I try to pass all of this into stories or books. If this happens to you as well and you can write on paper I would encourage you to do so, as the light from the screen of electronic devices can cause you to not be able to fall asleep as easily. Even if what you're thinking about is a short story or poem it's interesting to write it down and then read it in the morning. Sometimes it makes no sense but other times it is a super cool story or idea with a lot of potential.

The fun thing about experiences is that you usually get a few good stories out of them that you can tell anyone you meet. For example, when I was 14 years old I went on an exchange to Minnesota. The family I stayed with was unique in the sense that they had like 6 horses (literally in the woods that were their backyard) and only ate organic food. Both of these things were quite a shock as I was living in the countryside and I grew up in the city. I didn't even know what organic food was, this was over 10 years ago when eating healthy wasn't even a trend. The part I thought was weirdest was that my exchange sister had never tried McDonald's or Coca-Cola ever in her life. Can you believe that? At first I thought they were messing with me but it was real, I don't think I've ever met another person who has never had anything from McDonald's. Also, my exchange dad didn't understand a word I said because my accent was very different from theirs, which made communication difficult but we ended up getting along well since neither of us talked much.

While I was remembering this story I realized that my minimalism tendencies might have begun even before I realized as I didn't buy more than 4 clothing items during the 3 months I spent there and that was only because I needed a winter coat. When do you think you started becoming a minimalism? Either by wanting to adopt the lifestyle or just reduced your belongings.

If you have an interesting story about an experience in your life you can send me an email to **valentinapalermov@hotmail.com** I love reading interesting stories.

It is also important to understand how lucky we are, which is something we tend to forget but that is hard to ignore if we are visiting a place that has a lot of poverty. I am aware I have been blessed with being able to do a lot more than most people, which also inspires me to help and give back to those who weren't as lucky as me. There's people in this planet who don't have access to clean water or who can't afford food. If you can afford to eat 3 times per day if you want to then you're already richer than you think, this would be a luxury for over 40% of people in some developing countries. Buying a meal for a homeless person might not make a difference in your budget but it could be the only food they have access to that day. Helping those in need counts as an experience as well, as it helps you become more humble and it makes you think about how much you actually have and how little you actually need.

In the past few years I've dedicated a lot of my time to self improvement and one time I came across a video by one of my favorite people to listen to. I love watching and listening to videos and podcasts because it allows me to make the time I spend driving places more productive. There are a variety of ways to learn, experiences are an example but listening to other people's experiences is even better because you don't need to go through what they went through in order to gain knowledge. He was talking about how giving people in need a dollar can help them as much as it can help you. When you give a dollar (or more) to someone who needs it, you're training yourself to think in terms of abundance. You feel better when you help others and at the same time it is telling your brain that you have enough to share. Yes, they might buy something that's not necessarily good for them but that's not your fault, you did what was in your capacity to help. Plus, if you fear they're going to buy drugs with that money, you can always offer to buy them something to eat or give them food instead of money. Even if you don't have any money to give you can be generous with your time, which is your most valuable asset and resource, by helping them in some way. Use it wisely as you can't get it back. Be grateful for what you have and help others if you are able to.

CHAPTER 14: SKILLS

"By doing nothing, you become nothing."

- Unknown

Skills are valuable, things devaluate. Skills are based on knowledge, which compounds in value over time. Since it's knowledge, it cannot be taken away from you either unless you stop learning and forget because of not keeping the knowledge fresh, so keep renewing your abilities and connecting them with new ones. If you spend $500 on a course that's going to teach you how to paint and you end up selling $1,500 worth of paintings and making $500 in profit then that course just paid for itself and taught you a skill you can keep using to make money. If you buy a $500 coat, well… it's going to look very pretty and it'll be worth close to nothing in 5 years. This doesn't mean you shouldn't have nice things as that can add to your happiness as long as you don't end up letting it control your life.

Skills are an investment as they add value to you. What's the reason why some people get paid more than others? Simple, they have a more valuable skill set. People who go to college usually earn more than those who don't, and those who have work experience and/or a college degree can opt for a higher salary. The only reason why someone is making $10 per hour is because they haven't put in the work to increase the value they can provide. 10 years at a job doesn't mean you've become better at it, it usually means you've spent 10 years doing the same thing.

Let's take someone who works as a teacher as an example. Let's say you teach Kindergarten, you love kids and spend 10 years working with them. You figure out what works with them in the first 1-2 years and then keep using that strategy to teach them for the next 8-9 years. Your pay remains the same as your value input stays the same. You love your job and you don't need the money so you stay happily working with the children who join that school.

Now let's take the example of a teacher who wants to keep learning and growing, not that there's anything wrong with the other teacher. This one is just different. You teach Kindergarten and since you love kids you plan to spend at least the next 10 years working with them. You figure out what works with them in the first 1-2 years of teaching Kindergarten, then you ask for a promotion and offer to help train the next teacher who will be teaching Kindergarten. They accept your offer and you become a 6th grade teacher. Your pay is better but you also learn that it is tougher to deal with 6th graders than with little kids. It takes you 3 years to understand how to interact with them in the best way at the same time as teaching efficiently so that they learn better and develop more knowledge. The Principal is impressed with your abilities and decides to make you the Vice-Principal. Here you have access to information received from all the different grades in school and notice a pattern which could help the teens learn 2x faster if it is implemented while they're still in 1st grade. The principal and school board are a little skeptical about this new method so you decide to follow your hunch and start your own school after 4 years of working as Vice-Principal. The first year is a bit challenging but you find a way to make it work and by year 10 you are the Principal of your own school. It might have taken a lot more work but this teacher ended up in a very different position than the first one.

You might be wondering what this has to do with minimalism, but bear with me. How did the lives of these two teachers end up being so different? They started at the same place after all. Of course there are a ton of factors we are not taking into consideration but this is just an illustrative example. Well, one had the desire to grow and the other one didn't. And this is one huge lesson: whatever it is we are doing, time is going to pass anyway. So make the most out of it.

Growth is an essential part of life, we need it in order to continue feeling accomplished throughout our lives. When you finish something you have been working on you actually get a high from it similar to the one you would experience by doing other fun activities or even using drugs but on a lighter level since the chemicals released in your brain are similar.

If you aren't convinced yet, let's look at this as if money was not involved. Wouldn't you like to help others? Well, that needs skill as well. If you want to be a coach or anything else that's similar to that you not only need training but you also need the experience in order to help other people the best you can and actually make a difference in their lives. Let's assume you do not have any certification, you can still help them but this is going to require that natural skill and will to help others.

There are some skills which you can practice on a daily basis that you might not even consider as something "concrete" but which will end up making a huge difference in your life and how you see the world. Here I will share three of them which have impacted my life the most.

Meditation: Meditation is a skill you can use to calm down in 20 minutes if you're going through a stressful situation. This helps at a cellular level, specially in a world when we're always on the go. It is important to take a time out every once in a while and make an assessment of everything that's going on and how you plan to deal with certain situations and even give more thought to how you're going to achieve certain goals. Starting to practice meditation might be hard since we're not used to concentrating on not thinking or on thinking about just one thing or concept. The best thing you can do is to start. Even if it is just 4 minutes of silence it is going to make it easier to meditate for a longer time in the future. Take it as a skill that could change your life and make you more efficient and give it the necessary time to flourish before you give up.

Mindfulness: Be mindful of how you're living your life, the resources you're using and your effect on the people you meet. Live in the now, living in the past causes depression and living in the future causes anxiety. Being mindful works as an anchor to the now and brings you into the present moment, which will help you appreciate simple things such as how nice the weather is or how delicious the food before you smells and tastes.

Gratefulness: Being able to be grateful is a skill, and as any other skill, practicing it more often will make it easier to incorporate in your daily routine. This is something we don't really stop to think about because we get used to our way of living but if you start thinking about it, you're luckier than a lot of people. You have a home and food to eat every single day, as well as access to drinkable water anytime you're thirsty.

Skills require time, and time is expensive but sometimes we enjoy the activity we're doing so much that we don't even notice how much time we're spending on something. If you find an activity and skill worth your time that you also enjoy, you will effortlessly dedicate a big chunk of time to it. The trick is to find these activities as soon as you can in your life so that you have more time to dedicate to perfecting them rather than wasting time on other activities such as entertainment that even if they're fun, won't be adding that much to you as a person.

For me, you should find skills which you love in the different important areas of your life and invest time in them. These areas are health, happiness and value. The best scenario you can find is a skill which involves all of these. If not, one that will keep you healthy, one that makes you happy and one that increases the value you can give to this world.

CHAPTER 15: MORE TIME

"Be content with what you have; rejoice in the way things are. When you realize there is nothing lacking, the whole world belongs to you."

- Lao Tzu

Have you noticed some people just run around for the sake of feeling busy? But busy doesn't necessarily mean productive. We have somehow learned to associate busyness with hard work and at the same time forgot how to actually enjoy free time. And by free time I don't mean laying on the couch watching TV shows and having to sit through advertisements that are trying to sell you products to solve problems you weren't even aware you had. I need you to realize that your free time could be spent in anything. You could start a passive income business, write a book, read a book, watch educational videos on Youtube, get a mentor and talk to him or her, take a walk through the park to spend some time with yourself, as I said, it could be anything.

Getting more time is simple, eliminate the activities which you would rather not be doing and aren't important so that you can free up your time to do other activities.

Part of the problem is that that time is being spent in unfulfilling activities that end up not adding anything to your life. Time wasted doing something you enjoy isn't wasted time as you actually enjoyed it, just make sure you do enjoy the activity if it's considered as a time waste. It honestly seems like some people are actually scared of free time. Some people don't even use all of their vacation time!

So the real question is, how can you spend your free time doing something that makes you happy? Which activities do you find fulfilling?

Time is money. Well, actually money is time. Most people (knowingly or not) put a price tag on their time. If you accept a job that pays you $10 an hour then you're agreeing to that valuation of your time. Now, a really scary way of talking yourself out of buying a $300 pair of sneakers is to think that if you get paid $10 per hour, that means you would have to work 30 hours to be able to buy that pair of sneakers. That's more than a day worth of non stop work just to get shoes! However, if you were making $300 a week from a side hustle which you don't really pay attention to because you started it as a hobby then your hobby would be paying for your expensive taste. More interestingly, if you invested those $300 to generate a third stream of income, that third stream of income could give you enough return to buy that pair of shoes without sweating it. The key is to be able to delay gratification in order to get a bigger prize further down the line.

Don't be afraid to start your own business even if it's just a side business, specially if it is online and includes one of your passions (such as minimalism itself). These can turn into a semi-passive source of income.

Passive income is a topic that has gained a lot of traction in the last few years as it can help you in your journey towards financial freedom, and just freedom in general. It refers to the income you receive passively (without doing anything) after an initial investment of time and money. This keeps generating income even if you leave it unattended for months, something that would never be the case with a traditional job. Minimalism goes hand in hand with passive income because it frees up your time and energy to do what you enjoy. It also allows you to travel as it is usually not dependent on location so you can "work" from anywhere in the world as long as you have a phone or a computer and internet connection.

Be careful of what you choose to do with your time. Watching TV (Netflix and Youtube included), might be entertaining but it isn't really adding anything to your life unless it's something educational aligned with a skill that you want to develop, while investing your time building a business could mean retirement by the time you're 35.

Time is money and if you don't want to trade your time for money you need to learn how to make your money work for you.

If you could do anything you wanted, what would you be doing? When you wake up, in the middle of the day and when you go to sleep. How would you change the life you're living if you didn't have to work? Would you keep doing what you're doing?

It is important to find other activities to fill the time you've just cleared. Reading a book or inviting friends to your house are activities which actually increase your happiness and skills, even without noticing it. If you do not fill the time you've just cleared then it's most likely that you'll end up filling it with watching TV or going through Facebook/Instagram/Snapchat like you did before because you're not consciously using your time. You need to find activities which are beneficial for you such as exercising or learning how to play an instrument or even writing the book you've been thinking about since forever. This is why people who retire tend to die quicker, because they were used to occupying most of their time so when that stops, they don't know what else to do. Because they never learned what to do when they had free time. This is also one of the reasons why it's important to take your vacation time and more time off the office if you work a 9 to 5, to get used to having breaks to change activities and learn new things.

I usually change activities when I want to rest, so going to the gym is actually resting because I'm not putting a lot of mental effort into thinking what to write and actually writing and editing. Same when I come back from the gym and continue working on my book, since it's a switch in the activity I actually feel like I'm resting even though I just switched from one productive activity to the other. Even switching from writing one book to writing another feels like a switch in activity which I like to use to trick my brain into thinking it's resting. I'm not going to lie to you, I do spend some time watching series I enjoy, but that's the key point. Only those which I really enjoy are the ones deserving of my time, if I'm not particularly enjoying an activity which isn't particularly good for me, I change it in some way. If the series I'm watching is too boring, I just switch to another one or listen to music.

Make sure the activities you use to fill your time are aligned with your goals. You'll get there faster. And that if you're learning by reading a book or listening to a seminar that you actually implement the knowledge you're getting from it.

CHAPTER 16: MORE ACCOMPLISHMENTS

"It is preoccupation with possession, more than anything else, that prevents men from living free and nobly."

- Bertrand Russell

The way you decide to use your time is your decision to make. Although if what you want to achieve is to be happier and a better person, your free time should be dedicated towards making you a better person and working towards your goals.

Even if you hit your goal yesterday it doesn't mean you can just rest today. Being consistent is essential when it comes to hitting your goals and becoming successful.

Remember the list you made in one of the first chapters of where you wanted to be? It is time to take that list and divide it into smaller, achievable goals. If you set yourself a daily goal that's aligned with your long term goals, you will eventually achieve them. It doesn't matter how big they are. As long as you take a step everyday, you will be one step closer. Over the course of a year you will most likely be reaping the rewards of having stayed consistent.

In order to become more accomplished you need to set your goals and stick to them. You need to make a commitment to yourself that you're going to work on them as often as possible and also another commitment that you're going to word towards the same goal. Do not let yourself be distracted by shiny new opportunities along the way. You were the one who chose this path, now it is time to follow it. Before I pursue a new opportunity I ask myself if I'm willing to dedicate at least 3 years of my life to it. If the answer is no, I don't even consider going forward. If the answer is yes, I ask myself if I'm willing to commit 5 years. If the answer is yes, I pursue it. However I make sure I stay consistent with my other goals. Stop jumping from opportunity to opportunity, you will lose more time in the transition as well as how long it takes you to learn a new ability. By the time you're starting to see results you'll want to switch to the next big thing. But it is that specific time in which you start seeing results that you should be aiming to dedicate even more time to the activity as it means the business model has been proven. Now it's only time to find a way to scale it.

Same happens with exercise. If you want to have a toned body and a low fat percentage, it will not matter if you go to the gym for 3 hours, 4 days per week if you're not eating well on the other days. You can't compensate for a bad diet with exercise. It is similar to the "living below your means" scenario. If you have a calorie surplus, you will end up gaining weight. Only by being consistent with your exercise and a healthy diet will you eventually reach and maintain the body you want. As time goes by it becomes easier as you form habits that keep you in the road of success. And the longer you stay on it, the easier it is to get back. However if you see yourself drifting away, use all your effort to get back in line before it is too late.

Set a goal, this has to include the time frame and some way of measuring it. For example if my goal is to become a millionaire in the next three years the goal would look something like this: I will make $1,000,000 per year (measure) by 2021(time frame) with passive income on Amazon (what you're giving in exchange for the money). It seems unreachable doesn't it? Well, it's only because it's such a big number and three years doesn't feel like that much time. So the next step is to break it down, first by year and then into actionable steps you can take every week or every month. If you plan to double your income every year then you start breaking it down until it tells you how much you should make on the current year. Also, income is usually an exponential function if you're investing and a linear function if you have a job.

2021: $1,000,000 per year, 2020: $500,000 per year, 2019: $250,000 per year

2018: $125,000 per year, $10,417 per month, $2,605 per week

How much are you currently making per year and per month? Now it's about finding a way to reduce the gap between your current situation and your goals.

CHAPTER 17: BETTER HEALTH

"A healthy attitude is contagious, but don't wait to catch it from others."

- Tom Stoppard

Let's face it, keeping a healthy diet and exercising often are necessary if you want to have good health. In the past decade, America and other nations of the world have been experiencing a healthcare crisis. The obesity rate in America, Mexico and England have risen to almost half of their population. This and other factors have contributed to a sharp rise of the cost of treating diseases directly related to poor eating habits and a sedentary life.

Health is one of those things for which you have to make time now if you don't want to pay a huge price later.

You could argue that living minimalist life puts you in the road that leads to a healthier life. You might feel this chapter goes a little bit off topic, however it was necessary to include it as the consumerist behavior can be seen present even in this area.

There are tons of different ways in which you can exercise in order to keep your body healthy. In order to find what you enjoy, I suggest you try out different activities.

EXERCISE

- GYM: Of course, there are the people who enjoy going to the gym, like myself. While others find it extremely tedious and boring. The advantage of going to a fitness center is that you have access to a lot of different machines which you can try and alternate between. There's no limit on how much time you can spend there or which days you can go as they're usually open for many hours every single day. You also get access to classes like pilates or yoga which are included in your membership so that you can alternate and try them out before deciding if you actually want to continue going. Some gyms even have a pool so if swimming is something you enjoy doing, definitely join one of those. The cons are that you have to pay a monthly membership which might be cheap or expensive depending on where you live. You also have to drive to the place and designate a time for this depending how far your gym is.

- HOUSE GYM: The house gym is a like a miniature version of the gym. Meaning you will probably have a lot less equipment than what you'd find at a normal gym, however you can use it from the comfort of your own home. The pros are that you don't have to leave your house and can exercise at anytime during the day or night if you want to do so. The cons are that you actually need to own all of the equipment necessary, which kinda goes against the principles of this book.

- OUTDOOR ACTIVITIES: This is probably the best option for minimalists as it requires no equipment and you can do it anywhere in the world. You can walk, run, play volleyball or even do yoga at the park, it depends on what you like to do.

Now on to the diet part, it is essential that you aim towards eating more natural foods and cut back on processed and fast food.

DIET

Eating healthier isn't more expensive than eating junk food, you just don't know how and where to shop this type of food for it to be cheaper. This is a learning curve you will have to go through (or investigate on the internet before going) if you want to change your life for good. The positive side is that once you've learned from which place it is cheaper and faster to get everything you need, you will have that knowledge forever and it'll be easier for you to know what and where to shop. The other learning curve you're going to have to go through if you don't currently eat healthy is the one in which you learn which healthy foods are the ones you actually enjoy and how to cook them.

If you've been following the minimalism trend for a while you might have noticed a lot of minimalists become either vegans or vegetarians. You don't necessarily need to become a vegan if you want to become a minimalist but there are some lifestyle changes that you can implement to your lifestyle which will change it dramatically. Also, just because it's healthy doesn't mean it has to be boring or bland. I encourage you to find those healthy foods that you actually enjoy eating.

- Eat more fruits, vegetables and whole grains.

- Reduce your consumption of processed foods, meat, fast food, soda and cow milk. You can find healthier alternatives such as fresh food, organic meat, water or tea and almond milk.

- Stop eating sugar if you can. Sugar is more damaging to our bodies than fat and it is usually hidden in foods we don't expect it to be in. My skin has always been relatively clear and I've never had problems with acne, even when I was growing up and going through puberty TMI I know. But there was a time in which I started eating more packaged food since they were convenient to carry with me. After around 2 weeks I noticed my cheeks started to look horrible and I realized it was the amount of sugar contained in the snacks. Even after I stopped eating them, it took at least two months for my skin to clear up.

- Try buying seasonal fruits, these are a lot cheaper and much fresher than the ones that are not naturally growing at this time of the year or that have to be imported from very far away.

- Go in with a list of what you're planning to buy and stick to it as much as you can. Supermarkets are experts on making you buy things on impulse so having the willpower to stick to the list will save you a few bucks (and calories) every time you go in.

- Don't cut out the "bad" foods you enjoy entirely. If your favorite food is pizza, don't cut it out just because it is unhealthy, save it for a special occasion or find a healthier alternative such a cauliflower crust. Restricting can cause you to develop an unhealthy relationship with food and will make you crave that forbidden food even more. Suddenly you're obsessed with pizza and can't think about anything else, so you end up eating too much of it.

- Develop a healthy relationship with food. Life is too short to spend your time fearing food or avoiding everything with sugar in it, just learn how to eat more sensibly.

There's another important topic we must go through when talking about food. What is your relationship with it? It might be shocking to you but most people do not have a healthy relationship with food. We eat when we are stressed, happy, anxious, angry, sad, etc without asking our body if it is actually experiencing hunger. We use food as entertainment rather than for what it's meant to be consumed for: nutrients and energy.

Before your next meal try asking yourself if what you are going to eat is actually going to be beneficial for you and if you're hungry or just bored. Are you craving sugar, carbs or fats? Or would you be content with eating broccoli with hummus? Be aware of your portions as well as even if you're eating healthy it could lead to weight gain. If your body burns 2,000 per day and you consume 3,000 calories, you'll almost certainly gain weight. Even if you're consuming 3,000 calories of fruits, lean meats and whole grains.

Food and meal times is something we should be enjoying, that I'm not going to deny. However, you can still enjoy healthy meals with tons of veggies. Reserve fast food and other not-as-healthy options for a treat. Believe me, you will enjoy them a lot more than if you're having them every single day. Some people like to call it a cheat meal or cheat day but I don't consider it as cheating, just as a way of remaining sane.

NATURAL MEDICINE

The main goal of Pharmaceutical companies is to make money and they price their products accordingly as they have to absorb different costs such as research and development and operational costs. I'm not saying that their products don't work, they do work but there are sometimes in which they're just too expensive and a lot of people go into debt trying to finance their health.

It is no surprise that alternative treatments have become more popular. There's also a monetary benefit when selling and recommending these products but they tend to be more affordable and you don't really need a prescription for most of them as their side effects aren't as severe in most cases. Whatever it is you have or get in the future, I'm sure there's an alternative treatment for it.

Medicine has a lot of chemical ingredients which can be harmful to the body. I won't tell you to stop using medicine as it is a fast way to cure yourself, however it is not sustainable in the long run because of the side effects. I personally have nothing against modern medicine and had it not been for it, I could've died. I got pneumonia as a teenager and it was horrible and it wasn't until I started the treatment for it that I felt like I could breathe (Pun, anyone? No? Okay). In this case there was a factor of urgency which had to be addressed, and even if I swear by garlic, no amount of garlic would've gotten me out of the awful situation I was in, at least not as fast as I needed it to.

So learn how to balance and use both natural treatments and medicine in your favor and when the situation asks for it.

CONCLUSION: SIMPLICITY

"Simplicity is the most difficult thing to secure in this world; it is the last limit experience and the last effort of genius."

- George Sand

Simplicity refers to how all these concepts we have seen through the book integrate in your life. You want to aim for a life that's as simplified as possible so that you can free up your valuable time. This doesn't mean you don't have to do anything all day but that you can now do whatever it is you want with your time and spend it more productively as all the non essential activities are being taken care of automatically or have been eliminated completely from your life.

Simplicity in your Belongings

Own and keep only the things which are useful and make you happy. Think twice before acquiring a new item and don't hesitate to cut out what's not adding to your life.

Simplicity in your Finance

Automate your payments so that you're always on top of paying your bills and don't even have to think about them. Set up an automatic savings account if you can, saving money without having to do it yourself will help you save a bigger amount as you won't even notice the money is being saved. Pay off debt, preferably the one with the highest interest rate first. Find at least one source of passive income and work towards growing it until it makes you a decent amount of money per month.

Simplicity in your Wardrobe

Build your wardrobe around few basic items in your favorite colors and stick to a color scheme. Everything will match and you won't have to spend time thinking about it or changing outfits 10 times in the morning. Reduce your items to those that fit you perfectly and that you enjoy wearing.

Simplicity in your Lifestyle

Optimize your life for maximum productivity. Create a morning routine. If the first thing you do in the morning is roll over in your bed and check your phone, there's something you need to change. Morning routines will help you start your day energized and set yourself up for success.

Set goals. Something similar to that which everyone does in New Year but with a date so that you can hold yourself accountable. Now that you have your goals, break them down into monthly, weekly and daily activities that you have to do in order to hit them.

Have a productivity planner that you use daily. Productivity planners can mark the difference whether you achieve your goals or not. In here you will include your daily actions towards your goals. I use my productivity journal everyday and it has been a great help in keeping me accountable for what I commit to do during that day. I made my own productivity planner after trying out different formats for months, if you're curious what it looks like and you'd like to get it, this is the link to it:

https://www.amazon.com/Productivity-Planner-Plan-achieve-goals/dp/1983281883/ref=sr_1_1?s=digital-text&ie=UTF8&qid=1533408631&sr=8-1&keywords=productivity+planner

You can also search Productivity Planner Valentina Palermo on Amazon to find it. Or if you would like to get another one there are a lot of alternative options on Amazon as well.

It is essential that the goals you set for yourself align with your daily to-do list and there's at least one item in your to-do list that relates directly to each one of your goals. For example, one usual day for me includes writing at least 1,000 words for the book I'm currently working on, going to the gym and eating healthy.

Work towards your dreams. You need to have a reason why you're doing this. If your why is strong enough, you won't even need motivation as this will drive you to complete your daily goals every single day. Maybe you want to quit your job to see your daughter grow up or lose weight because of a health condition. Whatever it is, use it to push you forwards.

Exercise often. This will improve your mood and give you more energy, at the same time as improving your physical strength and looks.

Eat a balanced diet. Eating healthier will help you feel and look better. Of course, balance is key so if you want to eat pizza once a month there's no harm in doing that. The problem arises when you eat pizza everyday as you can't out-run a bad diet.

Give back. If you were able to buy this book with a credit card online it means that you have a card, connection to the internet and a device in which to access the Amazon website. This means you are most likely to be doing well in life, be grateful for it and give back to those who don't have the same luxuries as you.

A FEW WORDS FROM THE AUTHOR

Hello there, I'm Valentina and I would like to thank you for having read this book and for giving me some of your valuable time.

I hope you found its contents valuable and that you enjoyed reading it. If you would like to tell me what you thought personally you can send me a message to **valentinapalermov@hotmail.com** and I'll do my best to reply soon. I love hearing people's personal stories and anecdotes with minimalism or if you'd like to read about a topic in general I'd also love to know what that is.

The motive of this book is to tie minimalism and self development a bit so that you can live the best life possible in all regards and I do hope you found at least something which will help make your life a little bit better than before.

Thank you again for your attention,

Valentina

Printed in Great Britain
by Amazon

73164602R00051